THE RECITED
SPATES OF
LIMERICKA
(revisited)

THE RECITED SPATES OF LIMERICKA

(revisited)

A COLLECTION OF HUMOROUS AND SOCIAL
COMMENTARY LIMERICKS BY THAT LITTLE
KNOWN MASTER OF RHYME—

Martin C. Mayer

Order this book online at www.trafford.com
or email orders@trafford.com

Most Trafford titles are also available at major online book retailers.

Printed in the United States of America.

ISBN: 978-1-4669-0979-3 (sc)
ISBN: 978-1-4669-0981-6 (hc)
ISBN: 978-1-4669-0980-9 (e)

Library of Congress Control Number: 2011963571

Trafford rev. 01/05/2012

 www.trafford.com

North America & International
toll-free: 1 888 232 4444 (USA & Canada)
phone: 250 383 6864 ♦ fax: 812 355 4082

PREFACE

The limericks contained herein are the product of
the author's attempt to make his readers smile while
he pokes some fun at life's happenstances.

The "opinions" expressed herein (and each limerick is an
opinion) are strictly those of the author as he considers
the humorous possibilities of each subject matter.

In addition to being strictly his own jaundiced opinions, any
similarity to people, places or things which sound vaguely familiar
should be overlooked by the reader because they are intended
to be purely coincidental and a harmless effort to poke fun.
So, read on, and CONSIDER YOURSELF POKED!

ABOUT THE AUTHOR

Martin C. Mayer is a lifelong resident of The Garden State who recently retired to Palm Beach County in Florida.

His former career encompassed the practice of law, owning and operating a retail super market chain, constructing office buildings and shopping strips as an owner-builder, owning and operating a commercial lease auditing firm, and speculating in land on the peripheries of population growth.

Not a golfer, not a joiner, and only a mediocre tennis player, he now spends much of his retirement time penning limericks, odes, and other works of redeeming social commentary.

His most recent prior book is a humorous diary about Sunbelt retirement and is entitled "THE LAST LAP." Other writings by this author include "POETRY OF MIDLIFE CRISIS" and the original "THE RECITED SPATES OF LIMERICKA."

He readily owns up to being an I.L.I. (Ivy League Illiterate) despite B.A. and J.D. degrees from Columbia University. He rarely reads the writings of others, claiming he is too preoccupied manifesting his own creativity in curmudgeon-like fashion. He humbly hopes that you enjoy this book of his original limericks and refer to it whenever you begin to take the world too seriously!

LIPOSUCKERED

A lady with bottom too rounded
Liposuctioned, which left her dumbfounded:
So reduced was her mass
She could not find her ass,
So when seated could never be grounded!

END GAME

Parents with bipolar descendants
Often end up their children's defendants:
Their perspective is skewed,
So you're royally screwed,
And there just is no hope for ascendance!

DEFLATTIO

A guy with humongous kehonies
Placed a two million bet on the ponies;
This rendered him broke
In one masterful stroke,
Et reductio testiclonies!

GOLD WHO?

Hi ho, SILVER, I say!
It's the consummate investment metals play:
'Cause I've never been in danger
With the Margin Loan Arranger;
It's been up high, Oh SILVER, and AWAY!

NEVER ON HYUNDAI

There once was a high end car snob,
For Mercedes her poor heart did throb;
But once on a Monday
She drove a new Hyundai,
Now does gladly with peons hob nob!

SINK THE SHRINK

Dr. Bhil, I opine, is misguided:
Hears sob stories from families divided;
'Tho it's clear from the start
He should keep them apart,
With his fart he makes them reunited!

PI EYED

My friend Dom's a numerical goad
'Cause with math riddles he doth explode;
But one day, in his car,
His math went ajar;
By the numbers ranDom off the road!

RES ADJUDICATA

They say: "Courts will administer justice,
Bring your case to our firm; you can trust us;"
Then they file your plea,
Court adjudicates controversy;
That they can't tell the DIFFERENCE disgusts us!

CIALISY FALLACY

If your erection lasts more than four hours
You possess supernatural powers!
You don't need Cialis
To stiffen you phallus:
What you DO need are ice cold showers!

SUCK UP, BROTHER

I suffered a waiter named Eric
Whose service was barely generic:
'Tho he tried to kiss ass
He just found it too crass
And gave up on required hysteric!

SNAKE EYES

Young lady gave rich guy a dissin'
To spend time with new poor guy for kissin';
Rich guy's heart did break
And he called her a snake
Who'd be so poor with no pit to hiss in!

CANINE CAPERS

My dog has a pedigree blotch:
I can't get him to cease sniffing crotch;
That instinct's ingrained
And cannot be retrained,
So he greets with wet nose in your notch!

A LOTTO NONSENSE

Fortune cookies can make a man wacky
With advices therein that are tacky;
So don't heed what they say,
Throw those fortunes away,
And just eat one when e're you feel snacky!

TAKE IT WITH A GRAIN OF SALT

There once was a druggie named Mack
Who found white table salt in his crack;
Furiously miffed
His supplier he stiffed
So must now smoke while watching his back!

VERDREHISMIR

My personal life is a mess
And is probably beyond redress:
What goes in one ear's
Out the other, I fear;
Can't remember I have CRS!

BANK ON IT

My bank has long lines, fore and aft,
In hard times and now much understaffed,
But they do compensate
My inexorable wait:
For interest they give me the shaft!

LOLLIPOP, LOLLYPOP

A candy store guy from Nantucket
Had a girlfriend who just couldn't suck it;
So, with stern reprimand
He snatched pop from her hand
And back in inventory he stuck it!

A BOY NAMED SUE

My lawyer spends full time in Court
Filing actions in contract and tort;
'Tho his rep is prestigious
He's just plain litigious;
For him compromise is no resort!

SWATSA MATTER

A housewife, while chasing a fly,
Had a murderous look in her eye;
'Tho one clearly could find
She meant death in her mind,
In her heart the thought was just good-bye.

COFLIGHTIS INTERRUPTIS

My hubby, Spaceman Dick, had a penis
While co-piloting spacecraft to Venus;
When the last one returned,
On reentry, dick burned;
Now we don't have a penis between us!

DAILY DOUBLE TROUBLE

Lined up at the gate but not started,
One nervous race horse loudly farted;
All thought 'twas the bell,
So like bats out of Hell,
When bell rang all were long departed!

LASS IS GRASS

A young lady, financially hounded,
Robbed a bank, leaving patrons astounded;
'Tho she stashed all the loot
The cops made hot pursuit
And both cash and cute ass were impounded!

FATAL ATTRACTION

I'm in love with a beauty named Venus,
And I'm seeking commitment between us;
But try as I may
It's the field she'll play,
'Cause she only has eyes for my penis!

NIFTY AND THRIFTY

I once had a great C.P.A.,
But I've taken my business away:
At the end of the day
The same things they both say,
But the tax service asks for less pay!

BUDGET THE BUDGET

Municipal spending needs limit,
But it's hard to know just how to trim it,
Because when you cut service
The public gets nervous,
So gouge not and just merely skim it.

THE FORE DIMENSION

My golf partner thinks his mind is young,
But I know he is coming unstrung:
'Cause one can plainly see
There's no ball on his tee
Both before and after he's swung!

TUNIS FISH

A stunning young wench from Tunisia
Has a repertoire that's sure to please ya:
You just have to ask
Since she's done every task,
But just pray that she doesn't disease ya!

THE COLOR OF CHASTE

When I told her I loved her
She then let me know
That by Heaven above her
She was pure as driven snow.
Then I saw driven snow on her New York street
And realized she's a lying cheat!

TWIT'S END

A cold camper with warming desire
Kept throwing new logs on his fire
'Til the flames leapt so high
They ignited the sky
And morphed into his funeral pyre!

LIQUOR'S THE KICKER

A bar patron soliciting drink
Imbibed 'til he saw elephants pink:
When his memory got hazy
The crowd said he went crazy;
Now he's sleeping it off in the clink!

SEZ WHO?

Friends say I've become a curmudgeon
And viva esprit I do bludgeon;
Getting down to tacks brass,
THEY'RE A PAIN IN MY ASS,
And my attitude's simply not budgin'!

PANT 'O MINE

They were doing a vigorous, sexy dance;
When the music got slower
She slowly dropped her pants.
"That's ABSURD ENTENDRE", I heard her say
As he nabbed her virginity anyway.

VACATION TIT ELATION

In those nude resort-type Shangrilas
Women prance about without their bras;
So, divert your gaze from those bouncing protuberances,
Or your wife will be renouncing
Your exuberances!

PATCHWORK

I finally quit smoking
When I used the little patch.
Now, I am no longer choking
From my guggle to my zatch!

WHAT DID I THINK I SAID?

A professor with erudite mind
Made research notes he couldn't find;
Despite subject agility
He had collating senility,
So his thesis was deaf, dumb, and blind!

WRITE OF RETURN

My car rental's a pain in the neck:
They alleged I returned rental wrecked;
I replied, after lease,
It went back in one piece,
Yet they forced me to write a big check!

PRESCRIPTION PAYMENT

You must pay what the drugmakers say;
Are they with murder getting away?
I do not get my thrills
Funding prescription bills,
But it helps my ills have a nice day!

IT COMPUTES

My grandson just couldn't be cuter,
He's a six year old whiz at computer;
So, when power fails
While I'm sending emails,
I rely on the kid to rebooter!

M.D. FOR ME

Skillful doctors are something we need
If from illness we wish to be freed;
But the cost of it all
Does my wallet enthrall
While causing my bankbook to bleed!

TOUCHE

A novice young fencer named Jack
Ended up with a foil in his crack;
When opponent starts dancing
And thrusting while prancing,
He'll never again turn his back!

SALT LICK

A camper without any gear
Often camped open air without fear,
'Till a bear bit his bottom,
Other parts, something got 'em;
So, now camping he never goes near!

HICKORY DICKORY

A woodpecker high in a tree
Pecked huge holes where no one could see;
Soon the tree took a fall,
Woodpecker and all;
What remained of the bird starts with "p."

HE KNOWS JACK

There was an old codger named Irv
Who frequently liked to self serve,
But his girlfriend got mad
'Cause she knew she was had
When he no longer did HER with verve!

THE OTHER'S MOCCASINS

To mind your own business is wise,
You can't see with the other guy's eyes;
You're free to disagree
Based on how far you see—
What you DON'T may come as a surprise!

MAN ON TOP

My friend, Girard, is a master baiter,
So brag feats inconceivable
But sooner or later
He'll respond with a BIGGER bubbameise
That's so believable
It's bound to surprise ya!

FOOD FOR THOUGHT

An insomniac craving more sleep
Made self promise he just couldn't keep:
He could not do away
With his Midnight buffet
'Cause his tummy declined such a leap!

SWINE AND BIER

There was a material bloke
Who fattened a pig in a poke;
He thought he would get
A huge price for the pet,
But he didn't, because the pig croaked.

BRAIN FRIEZE

We don't learn to come in from the rain
And repeat all those things that cause pain:
So, when after divorce
Or a new career course
That is why we choose wrong once again!

SECOND OPINION

Doc opined it was deep vein thrombosis;
She refused to heed his diagnosis:
She just didn't care
To face such despair
And believed she'd be cured by osmosis!

SHINGRILA

I've developed a bad case of shingles,
From guggle to zatch it all tingles;
There's no use in bitching,
It won't stop the itching
Or the pain that with itch intermingles!

DIABETES MELLITUS

We've been diagnosed with diabetes,
The affliction will not defeat us—
When you learn you are sick
Seek remedial shtick;
Thanks to insulin, it won't delete us!

LETTERFLY

A timid young man from New York
Was labeled by friends as a dork;
So he started anew
'Tho he hadn't a clue
And allowed EVERYTHING to uncork!

AIR WE DARE

New autos will run on thin air,
At least that's what I hear some declare;
But car proliferation
Might cause suffocation
If that left for breathing gets rare!

WHAT'S IPANA?

A Converso who hails from Costilla
Has bad breath that could level Godzilla:
When confronted about it
He replied "I don't doubt it,
Haven't brushed since the Spanish Flotilla!"

TV IS FLAT (ULENT!)

To TV big flat screens add dimension:
They command panoramic attention;
But I find I still shrivel
At the programming drivel
Of this conversation killing invention!

FLIPPING THE BIRD

A zookeeper in charge of the birds
With a parrot exchanged nasty words;
When the crowd overheard
This encounter absurd
THEIR OWN cursing could not be deferred!

RELATIVES ARE RELEVANT

Unless you are deaf, dumb, and blind
You are sure to have some ties that bind;
The essence of this
Should produce happiness
And not a kick in your behind!

SALINE SOLUTION

Hubby snores but yet denies;
Wife loses sleep, and so she cries;
Next day long, she's a sleepy head;
Next night long, in a different bed!

BREACH OF PREMISE

Philanderers lack real pride,
They have cast marriage vows to the side;
It is one thing to cheat
If you're reasonably discreet,
But don't act like you've nothing to hide!

ALTAR BOUY

Most people can't handle rejection,
It creates egotistical pain
And might lead to behavioral correction
To ensure it won't happen again!

HABEAS POSTERIAS

A Mexican guy named Gonzales
Clandestinely crossed at Nogales;
No Citizen Paper
Soon ended his caper,
And so no U.S.A. uber allis!

PIETY PROPRIETY

If you're pious, be pious all day,
Or else you with piety play;
So, comport it straight laced
And not double faced,
'Cause it's what you DO, not what you SAY!

OLD AGE E.D.

My hubby has old age E.D.,
But he claims he's just not "in to me";
Sad, that's literally true,
He has an unctuous skew
That avoids my shrill Viagra plea!

BURNED UP

I would like to live in an environ
That's devoid of the shrill fire siren:
In a civilized world
One should not get blood curled
Simply 'cause someone else has a fire on!

YES MEANS IMMEDIATELY

Whene're she doth ask me to sate her,
There is only one way to placate her:
Postpone? Hesitate?
NO, she simply won't wait:
Sooner has the same meaning as laider!

FOUNTAIN OF USE

Fire hydrants oft' take much abuse:
Dogs pee on them and plugs come loose;
City children at play
Sometimes romp in their spray,
But don't park at one—there's no excuse!

LOOK AWAY, JOSE

I try to avoid confrontations,
They don't fit my lifestyle plan,
But in spite of my own trepidation,
I find that FIT still hits the SHAN!

FIRE EXCHANGE IS NOT ROBBERY

An arsonist, peeved at his lover,
Vowed to burn her with clandestine cover;
He mixed stuff in a pot
Which exploded when hot;
Now it's HE who is pushing up clover!

NO CHARGE FOR THE TOPPING

A kid with a double dip cone
Was licking it with happy tone
When a bird in the sky
Topped his cone on the fly;
Oh, how quickly was happiness blown!

GENTLEMEN PREFER BLENDS

A shepherd who did it with sheep
Went to bed but could not fall asleep;
So nocturnally boring
Was animal scoring,
He soon called upon Little Bo Peep!

SEEKING APPSOLUTION

App phones just fire my unction,
There's an app for about every function;
I like talk, don't like tap
So avoid all the flap;
Will not buy one, I have great compunction!

PEW

While attending church services nightly
A parishioner perfumed impolitely.
Things did not auger well,
and because of the smell
Church attendance fell off more than slightly.

THINGS ARE NOW LOOKING UP

A limp football player from Dallas
Had his doctor prescribe him Cialis;
His scoring got better,
Won a varsity letter,
And now has a girlfriend named Alice.

THE BREADTH OF BREATH

Seignior Pedro talks right in your face;
You retreat, he advances in pace;
His accent is charming
But his breath's so alarming
You would gladly repel him with mace!

SHPILKAS

(Or: Nervous Energy)

'Tho I go to the spa for massage,
Relaxing's for me a mirage:
And so as I undress
To myself must confess
That my shpilkas will never dislodge!

KNITTING PRETTY
(Or: I've Got You Under My Skein)

A knitter with patterns ambitious
Creates work that is simply delicious;
But she cares not a twit
For the cost of the knit
And does ne'er find the task repetitious!

THONG AND DANCE

Some women wear thongs to the gym;
They believe it keeps pantyline trim;
But the view from the back
Accentuates crack
And distinguishes her from a him!

CURTAINS

When I go to the theater, I'm late,
I just never can get there by Eight.
'Tho I'M ready on time
My date spouts some sad rhyme
Which I never with truth can equate.

TAKING CHANCES

When I think of the chances I've missed
At myself I become sorely pissed;
I'm in charge of my fate
But I still hesitate:
Fear of failing is hard to resist!

KINDLEGARTEN

A clever device is the Kindle,
It will surely make hard copies dwindle;
So, give thanks on your knees
'Cause it saves banks of trees,
And the new price is hardly a swindle!

SCHOOL BELLE

In New Hope we met a cross dresser
Who professed he's a college professor;
Clearly his mind went spastic
Over all things scholastic,
But it wasn't our task to redress her!

DRUNKEN IS AS DRUNKEN DOES

A man from Pierre, South Dakota
Prefers drinking scotch without soda.
The reason, he tol' me:
"I get drunk much more slowly,
But HOW DRUNK won't change one iota!"

TIME WARP

A homeless man humbly implored us
For some funds as he kneeled before us;
But we learned 'twas a scam
And a tax free flim flam:
Five years later he tried to encore us!

CONVERSATIONAL GRACES

I would like to give social retraining
To my best friend's mode of entertaining:
His patter is boring,
Filled with brags and folkloring;
Net result: agitation ingraining.

VEY IS BEER

A Mennonite named Orsen Buggy
Wore undershorts that fit too snuggy;
So, when sneaking a beer
Realized his worst fear:
No expansion for his chugaluggie!

VACATION EVALUATION

We booked an excursion to Italy,
But the trip ended up rather shittily:
We forgot to go shopping
When the Euro was dropping
And were bored, so we didn't do diddily!

EL MUNDO NON SECUNDO

A first in line patron named Quillan
Kept cashier multi requests fulfillin';
Other patrons in line
On her mouth had design
But to shut her up no one was willin'!

AIRPORT DINER

As you enter the staff howdy doos ya,
It's a prelude to how they will screw ya:
Their menu's too pricey,
Their food fare is dicey;
When you're done, they with smiles toodle ooya!

T.S.A. AT THE AIRPORT

T.ough S.hit, A.merica,
Security's our aim,
So if you have a problem
It's the crazies you should blame!!

THANK GOODNESS

My car is a magnet for birds:
I'm forever removing their turds;
So I think I know why
Behemoths don't fly:
The problem would be too absurd!

WRITER'S ITCH

I have found myself scratching my but
As I've structure of sentence rethought;
As rethought gets replanned
I might scratch if or and
Until written perfection is wrought!

I CAN'T HEAR EWE

A shepherd had love for his sheep
And would count them out loud in his sleep;
Wife could take it no more
So she learned how to snore,
And his sounding of counting could bleep!

BONER

A man multi fractured his coccyx
When he fell while lifting big boxes;
Then he learned there's no cast
For the bone that comes last
And spate curses quite loud and obnoxious!

GENDER BENDER

Flirtation's female affectation,
It's really THEMSELVES that they please;
So, whenever they start,
Don't respond with your heart:
Cross your eyes when'ere they do their tease!

BLOW JOB

Clementine, suicidal inclina,
Stuffed explosives into her vagina;
She then lit the match
Which ignited her snatch
And blew her throughout Carolina!

V-D ENGINE

An old man with a vintage Bugatti
Gave joy rides to a very young hottie;
He had high expectations
For some intimate relations,
But that was not all that he gottie!

EMPLOYMENT PITCH

A flutist, a South Caroliner,
Plays melodically, major and minor;
At interview for a job
Her nerve endings would throb,
And soon playing off key did define her.

CHOOSERS SHOULDN'T BE BEGGARS

A beggar with hat in his hand
Chose a corner on which he did stand;
But the public was stingy
'Tho he counted on bingy,
And supply fell quite short of demand!

CREMATION IS THINKING GREEN

Cremation's a hot topic to talk about:
You must do it while you still can walk about.
At the risk of a pun:
Choose rare, medium or well done—
No costly dirt of coffin to squawk about!

STOPPED LIZTENING

A brilliant young pianist played Liszt
But bad showmanship couldn't resist:
After playing his quota
He kept replaying the coda
'Till his audience got sorely piszt!

PRAGMATIC ACCOMODATION

A lass with a needy vagina
Took a lover in North Carolina;
When he ended the tryst
She was mightily pissed,
But she soon found two more to reclina.

PERCEPTION BARRIER

When you think it's a reductio ad absurdum
First be certain you correctly heard 'em.
Don't be quick to reject
How the speaker reflects
'Til you figure out how YOU will wordem.

THE NOSE KNOWS

A cowboy who hailed from Montana
Had a nose that looked like a banana;
'Tho in constant denial
Of proboscis profile
He still hid it in his bandana!

MATHEMATICAL CONUNDRUM

When I add one plus two I get three,
A formula easy to see;
But the square root of twelve
My poor brain cannot delve
And does make me from math learning flee!

FLOWER POWER

A one legged florist called "Gimp"
Was known as an infamous pimp:
He spent countless hours
Arranging deflowers,
But one day his "business" went limp!

BATTLE OF THE BED

When he's sleeping he usually snores,
An occurrence she totally abhors;
So with elbow she gives a hard nudge,
But he gives encores
In a half sleeping grudge!

DEFAULT, DEAR BRUTUS,
IS WITHIN OURSELVES

You did not pay the mortgage, you cannot remit;
You've exhausted resources and pawned all your shit;
You've joined ranks of defaulters who just thumb their noses
And enjoy freebie housing 'til the lender forecloses!

TOOT OR BOOT

There are times when you should say your piece;
There are times when you should remain mute;
When your mouth is in play
You must know WHEN to say
Or you might in your ass get a boot!

WAVE LENGTH

A lass with a high strung libido
Lives her life attuned to her own credo:
She will offer romance
To whomever wears pants,
Be it jeans, undershorts, or tuxedo!

FD SOS

A huge fire in our high rise did swell,
Leaping flames like infernos in Hell;
The FD, I profess,
Heeded our SOS
And saved us all from SOL!

STENOSIS THROMBOSIS

When my vertebrae got misaligned
A spinal M.D. I did find:
But his M.R.I. bill
Caused spine columnar chill
And consulting fee just blew my mind!

UNSOCIAL NETWORKING

I cannot stand Facebook or Twitter:
They make modest man a big bullshitter!
So, if you're discrete
Never Twitter or Tweet
And spare us the internet litter!

MAN WITH A WHEEL LIFE PROBLEM

A genius with patents aplenty
Had a paranoid need to invente;
So, despite his ordeal
Reinventing the wheel,
He could not shake his strong malcontente!

SIZE MATTERS

A researcher with penile obsession
Unnerved a young priest at confession:
She said she did clone
Ones she hankered to own
And displayed her results at the session!

DISEASE CONTAINMENT

A klepto confined to a jail
Had a game plan he knew would not fail:
He would steal his own clothes
Out from under his nose
And, thus, no further charges entail!

TENNIS, THE MENACE

They played vicious, competitive tennis,
Each team vowed they would win at all cost;
Soon the score was a 40-Love menace,
But the final score was: No Love Lost!

EASY READER

Momma thought if young kids would read books
They would not end up ignorant schnooks;
So I read her Marriage Manual
And the Hustler Annual:
Then, SURPRISE, she let me off the hook!

HAD BURNS ASPIRED

O, wud the Power the giftie gie us
And Revelation just decree us!
That ain't the way the Lord would ha'e us,
And the very thought must be impious!

OF MICE AND MEN

The best laid married men and mice
Might still aft gang agley
To get themselves that promised joy
The griefless, painless way!

WHATSADILDO?

A lady employed large cucumbers
Whilst enjoying her afternoon slumbers;
She brought rapid orgasms
To all of her chasms
And quickly lost track of the numbers!!

DYSLEXIA AT THE CINEMA

I do remember way back when
In Theater 9 I savored "TEN".
But yesterday was less devine:
In Theater 10 I suffered "NINE".

SEX QUESTIONS AND ANSWERS

The question I must ask myself:
"Has she now put sex on the shelf?"
'Cause according to my Fortune Cookie,
I'm suffering from Lackanookie!

STOCK MARKET PROGONSTICATION

'Tho stock market's one big crapshoot,
Your stockbroker still gets HIS loot;
He can hold you or trade you
While profits evade you;
That's a postulate hard to dispute!

INTERSECTION SURVEILLANCE CAMERAS

If you ever a red light do pass
Photocameras will now catch your ass;
Despite ongoing litigation
Over rights violation
The drivers pay stiff fines en masse!

CHOOSING TIRES

Most car tires come stamped with a rating,
The value of which we're debating:
Because for a ride nice
You trust dealer's advice:
If he's wrong, it's too late and frustrating!

BLIND GROCERY ITEMS

Supermarkets can play this cruel game,
Be self righteous and deny all blame:
Think you're such a smart feller?
Just go buy a slow seller
And the price you'll pay's a crying shame!

"CHEAP" GENERICS

We are led to believe they are cheap
'Cause some drug stores just sing us to sleep:
But their MARKUP, I say,
Ought to cause you dismay:
It's a MUCH LARGER PROFIT they keep!

PUMPED UP

Gas pump prices are truly obscene
For a fuel that in no way burns clean:
It's not in short supply,
That's a transparent lie:
SPECULATORS are heard but not seen!

HERE COME DA JUDGE

A limerick's a beautiful thing,
It will humor to most readers bring;
If you've relished my joke
I won't go up in smoke
And be left with my ass in a sling!

WRITING SOCIAL COMMENTARY LIMERICKS CAN BE FUN!

Dear Reader:

Many thanks for purchasing this volume of my original humorous and social commentary limericks. This author believes that each of us has a limerick or two in us if we concentrate upon those experiences in life which amuse us, abuse us, or confuse us. Try sitting in a quiet place, let your mind wander, and lose yourself a bit, and soon the words you write will serve as a vehicle for getting your true feeling about the subject matter out of your system. Think of all the money and time you now will have saved on visits to the shrink and bicarbonate of soda! Also, the release of these pent up feelings in graphic form will result in a great sense of personal gratification and accomplishment.

Do not be discouraged. We have provided more than enough lined pages for you to revise your limerick a few times. The first several drafts of a limerick hardly ever "cut the mustard." So, if at first you don't succeed, (well, you know the rest!). GOOD LUCK!

Martin C. Mayer